Let This Radicalize You:
A Workbook

Published in 2023 by
Haymarket Books
P.O. Box 180165
Chicago, IL 60618
773-583-7884
www.haymarketbooks.org
info@haymarketbooks.org

ISBN: 979-8-88890-073-4

Distributed to the trade in the US through Consortium Book Sales and Distribution (www.cbsd.com) and internationally through Ingram Publisher Services International (www.ingramcontent.com).

This book was published with the generous support of Lannan Foundation, Wallace Action Fund, and Marguerite Casey Foundation.

Special discounts are available for bulk purchases by organizations and institutions. Please email info@haymarketbooks.org for more information.

Library of Congress Cataloging-in-Publication data is available.

Entered into digital printing May 2023.

LET THIS RADICALIZE YOU: A WORKBOOK

April 2023

This workbook is intended as an extension of our book *Let This Radicalize You*. It was created to feature resources that we couldn't fit in the book, including other helpful books, essays, wisdom from veteran organizers, and more.

Educator and activist Ursula Wolfe-Rocca drafted the "Souped-Up Study Guide," which is the core of this workbook. The other components are included as a supplement to the guide. We plan to use this workbook as part of a workshop series that we are facilitating in fall 2023. But we've designed it so that it can also be used by independent study groups and individuals outside of group settings.

Write and doodle all over this workbook, that's why it was created. We hope you find it useful as a resource. If so, make sure to tell others about it.

Our thanks to Ursula for her work, to Saiyare Refaei for her wonderful illustrations, to Anne Kosseff-Jones for her edits, and to Partner & Partners for designing this workbook.

In solidarity,
Mariame and Kelly

TABLE OF CONTENTS

PART I

6   Study Guide

10   Chapter 1: Beyond Alarm, Toward Action

15   Chapter 2: Refusing to Abandon

21   Chapter 3: Care is Fundamental

25   Chapter 4: Think Like a Geographer

32   Chapter 5: Rejecting Cynicism

38   Chapter 6: 'Violence' in Social Movements

44   Chapter 7: Don't Pedestal Organizers

48   Chapter 8: Hope and Grief Can Co-exist

53   Chapter 9: Organizing Isn't Matchmaking

60   Chapter 10: Avoiding Burnout

64   Conclusion: Relationships, Reciprocity, and Struggle

72   Conclusion: Beyond Doom, Toward Collective Action

73   Afterword: Movements Make Life

74   Closing Invitation

PART II

80   Reflecting on Ideas

84   Self-Reflection for Organizers

86   Movement Assessment Resources

88   Direct Actions

94   Activist/Organizer Wisdom

98   Bibliography

105   Other Useful Resources

STUDY GUIDE

About This Guide

The epigraph to *Let This Radicalize You* says, "Everything worthwhile is done with other people." That includes reading this book. This guide is written with the hope that you will be reading LTRY with other people-your friends, chosen family, comrades, co-strugglers, and co-organizers. Throughout this guide, you will be asked to reflect, analyze, and share-with an expectation that sometimes the *you* will be collective, and sometimes it will be singular. However, if you find yourself in an isolated place and you are reading this alone, that's OK too!

Another assumption of this guide is that you are already engaged in some form of organizing-no matter how small. If you are not sure if your actions toward building a more just world constitute "organizing," this book is also for you. There are many questions and prompts that encourage you to tailor your reflection to the specific circumstances of your political work. But if you are reading this book during a time of transition, you might think about work you hope to take up in the future or organizing you've done in the past.

This guide is also rooted in the understanding that reading is an active, potentially transformative process. The questions in the study guide are not meant to test your recall of the words in the text, but rather to invite you in to a process that includes both deep reflection and the coconstruction of knowledge with the authors, your comrades, and yourself. In LTRY, Ruth Wilson Gilmore talks about the dangers of "reading-as-extraction:"

> I realized that a good deal of the practice of reading that I brought to my work, my work as a scholar, my work as an activist, my work as a reader, was kind of extractivist in its character. I was reading things in order to pull something out that I could then use...that I could then hold up, like, I pulled this chunk of copper ore from the ground, see it? I pulled this other thing from the ground, see it? This extraction

> then left me with something I could show to people, "See, I have this
> copper ore, see, I have this sentence from Karl Marx," or sentence
> from Claudia Jones, or even an entire paragraph from C. L. R. James
> that I could recite. And people would just look and say, "Wow, that's
> really nice copper ore."

No doubt, this book is full of wisdom, stories, and quotations that you will want to share. May the sharing you do be in the service of analyzing your context, building sturdy relationships with others, organizing, and taking action-not merely marveling at shiny objects. *Let This Radicalize You* is a marvelous invitation to action; may this guide help you and your community of co-strugglers clarify how you might creatively, joyfully, defiantly-and again and again-answer that invitation.

Structure of the Guide

- **Prereading journal prompt** for each section/chapter. These writing prompts are intended to frame the reading to come. Always, you are encouraged to share your reflections with others and, in turn, deeply listen to their stories, reflections, and insights.

- **Reflection questions**. These questions are opportunities to pause, reflect, connect, and apply what you're reading. If you are reading with others, you might select a few to anchor your discussions. These can be answered in conversation with each other or in writing-or both. If you are not reading this in community, you might share questions and powerful reactions on social media (citing the authors and book) to invite the reflections of online comrades and friends. For each chapter, there is also a final invitation to jot down the additional questions that bubbled up and crystallized for you over the course of reading.

- **A take-it-with-you line**. The final question of each chapter is always the same: What is a line from this chapter that you want to share with others? Why? This final prompt reminds us that "everything worthwhile is done with other people." It also acknowledges that there are many poignant moments in this book that are not reflected in the study guide. This prompt encourages you to fill in the gaps of this guide.

Sharing Practice

If you are reading this book in community, it is worth spending some time carefully considering what norms or protocols you want to adopt for reading, sharing, discussing, and listening as you move through the book and guide together. In Chapter 9, "Organizing Isn't Matchmaking," Kelly and Mariame write:

> **Many people describe themselves as good listeners. In reality, most people are not. This disparity between perception and practice can be explained by the fact that most people think of being a good listener as a personality trait-like being friendly or upbeat. But while being a good listener may come more easily to some people than others, it is not, in fact, a mere personality trait. Like so many other aspects of organizing, listening is a practice...**
>
> **This society has not conditioned us to be attentive listeners. When people say things that make us uneasy or impatient, instead of listening we often hone in on what we want to say next or drift into contemplation of how the matter relates to our own plans or experiences. To stay in the moment with another person, to truly hear and consider what they are saying without slipping into reaction or retreating inward, can require intention.**

Without intention, small group discussions can fall into the same unhealthy patterns of the larger society, reflecting existing power relations of age, race, class, gender, sexuality, and disability-with some folks talking a lot while others stay quiet; interrupting or rushing to respond to each other; or failing to carefully listen to and engage with the specificity of a person's understanding and experience.

There is no one way to organize a reading or study group to ensure generative and equitable conversations, but establishing a reading and sharing protocol can provide a foundation that you can build upon and refine as you move through the text together. Some questions you might consider as you develop your protocol:

1 **At what rate will you move through the book?** Building in a check-in about pacing after the first couple of readings is helpful. Matching reading goals to members' capacity is vital for making a reading group sustainable.

2 **How might you build in both flexibility and accountability around reading?** Sometimes life happens and one literally cannot do the homework; at the same time, joining a book group requires some level of commitment to reading and reflection.

3 **How are you ensuring adequate processing time for all members?** Quieter folks often end up "missing" their chance to speak without sufficient time to reflect on and prepare what they want to say. Building in a few minutes of writing or sketching before verbal processing is one strategy that can broaden participation.

4 **How are you rotating the sharing structure?** Consider moving between different configurations of full group, small group, and partner sharing. To ensure the broadest participation possible, you might also rotate the order of sharing, so that the most eager to speak does not always go first.

5 **What roles do you need for each meeting and how will you rotate/ share them?** Roles may include facilitator, timekeeper, notetaker, etc. You might rotate facilitation of meetings so that different folks take turns anchoring the conversation.

6 **How are you making space for feedback on meeting facilitation and structure?** After the first couple meetings, it can be helpful to gather feedback from your group about what's working and what's not. It can be helpful to invite these responses, in writing, at the end of a meeting through a Google Form or similar document or survey everyone has access to. These reflections can be discussed and used to revise the meeting norms or structure.

FOREWORD BY
MAYA SCHENWAR
AND INTRODUCTIONS BY
KELLY HAYES
AND
MARIAME KABA

PREREADING JOURNAL PROMPT

In her foreword, Maya Schenwar recounts meeting Mariame Kaba for an interview on Prison Industrial Complex (PIC) abolition "in search of answers," but leaving with a brain "buzzing with questions upon questions." *What questions are you coming into this book with? What answers are you seeking?*

REFLECTION QUESTIONS

1. How does Schenwar's examination of the word "radical" (xi and xiii) match up with your own understanding of your (and/or your group's) politics?

2. Kelly shares lines from "Rant" (2–4) by Diane di Prima. You can read the poem at the link below. What lines resonate with you? Write (or sketch or paint) about some of your reactions.

evergreenreview.com/read/rant-from-a-cool-place/

3.   Kelly writes: *"...when you feel trapped by an oppressive inevitability, you never stop trying to escape, because every jailbreak begins with a decision to reject the inevitable"* (3). Consider your own context—experiences, histories, and identities. What are the oppressive inevitabilities you are working to reject?

4.   What is your response to Kelly's assertion that *"storytelling is a fight for the future"* (4)? What stories are you bringing to the fight?

5.   Explore Mariame's anecdote about "butterflies" (8). What do you recognize? What resonates? What are the takeaways for you and your work?

6.   Carefully study the paragraphs Mariame devotes to describing the Marissa Alexander case (10—12). What lessons might you borrow and apply from this example of organizing?

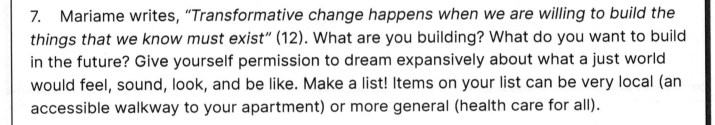

freemarissanow.org/about.html

7.   Mariame writes, *"Transformative change happens when we are willing to build the things that we know must exist"* (12). What are you building? What do you want to build in the future? Give yourself permission to dream expansively about what a just world would feel, sound, look, and be like. Make a list! Items on your list can be very local (an accessible walkway to your apartment) or more general (health care for all).

8.   According to Mariame, how are activism and organizing overlapping and different? How do these descriptions match up with the work you have been involved in?

9.   What additional questions came up for you as you read?

Take-it-with-you line:

What is a line from this chapter that you want to share with others? Why?

CHAPTER ONE
BEYOND ALARM, TOWARD ACTION

PREREADING JOURNAL PROMPT

Think about a time in your life when you took meaningful action, small or large, to seek more justice. This could be a time you worked on a campaign, organized or joined a protest, participated in mutual aid, or supported the organizing of others with your time, skills, money, or resources. Or perhaps it is an interpersonal example-a time you advocated for someone in your family or community, extended an apology to someone, or answered a call from a friend in need. What moved you from inaction to action, nonparticipation to participation? What is your best understanding of the circumstances that moved you to act?

REFLECTION QUESTIONS

1. Consider the campaign on behalf of survivors of police torture in Chicago. What lessons do you want to hold on to from this example of organizing?

chicagopolicetorturearchive.com/about

2. Kelly and Mariame state: *"Facts are not enough to mobilize people to action"* (19). Does this ring true to you? What are the circumstances that make it more likely that facts will be useful in moving people to action? Think back on your own experiences. Have there been times in your life when powerful facts helped move you to action?

3.   Building on Ruth Wilson Gilmore's story about her visit to Berkeley High School (22), think about the issues you are currently organizing around or hope to organize around in the future. What is a related story you want to lift up, one that will be an invitation, not merely an alarm?

4.   Learning from Shana McDavis Conway (29), what emotions, besides fear, might you tap into as you work to invite others to join your efforts? Make a list or chart of at least two emotions and explain why and how they might act as invitations to action.

5.   Mariame and Kelly write, *"Organizing gives us the opportunity to do more than map out the monstrosity that is the system; it allows us to build bonds between people in unique and powerful ways"* (33). Think about the bonds that connect you with your co-organizers and co-strugglers. In what ways are you interested in strengthening or growing these bonds? What are some actions you might take toward that goal?

6.   Replicate Dean Spade's thought experiment exercise: *"What if we just sat down and imagined in the most complex way we can, a plan for breaking people out of prison?"* (35). What is your plan? What did you learn from the process of developing the plan?

7.   What does "belonging" mean to you? When have you felt a sense of belonging? The absence of it? How are you and your comrades deliberately building spaces that foster belonging-or how might you in the future?

8.   What additional questions came up for you as you read?

Take-it-with-you line:

What is a line from this chapter that you want to share with others? Why?

CHAPTER TWO
REFUSING TO ABANDON

PREREADING JOURNAL PROMPT

Savior and hero narratives are ubiquitous in U.S. popular culture and are inescapable in fields like social work and teaching. They can also show up in our approaches to organizing. Think back to your own experiences. Have you encountered saviorism in yourself or others? If so, what was its impact on the relationships and/or goals of your work?

REFLECTION QUESTIONS

1.   Monica Cosby powerfully reformulates the common phrase "light at the end of the tunnel" as "we were all in the tunnel just making light" (42). What strikes you about this reformulation? What else stands out to you about the story she tells? What does it truly mean to refuse to abandon each other?

2.   Where in your life and community do you see "people merely cooperating with the world as they understand it"? What does it mean to "live in opposition to abandonment" rather than judge "them for their failures and release ourselves from any further obligations toward them" (45—46)? What are some ways you already (or might in the future) practice "living in opposition to abandonment"?

3.   Ejeris Dixon says, "If you show up for people, they show up for you" (46). How do you want to show up for your fellow organizers? How do you need them to show up for you?

4.   Dixon describes a process of relationship- and base-building rooted in questions and genuine curiosity. Which of her questions are most powerful to you? Which might you borrow for your work and context?

5.   Kelly and Mariame note that "we do not need heroes" but that "the importance of saving others should not be dismissed" (52). How is the ethic and fact of interdependence different from the idea of saviors and saviorism?

6.   Many of the "acts of rescue" described in this chapter are "essential, but not extraordinary" (55). What are the essential-but-not-extraordinary goals of your organizing or work?

7.   What additional questions came up for you as you read?

Take-it-with-you line:

What is a line from this chapter that you want to share with others? Why?

CHAPTER THREE
CARE IS
FUNDAMENTAL

PREREADING JOURNAL PROMPT

Write or sketch: *What does care feel like? Sound like? Taste like? Smell like? Act like?* You might respond based on a real-life example or imagine something you've not yet experienced.

REFLECTION QUESTIONS

1.   The opening pages of this chapter describe three different examples of "mass activation events"—Hurricane Maria in Puerto Rico, the COVID-19 pandemic, and the police murder of George Floyd. Consider these (or similar) events and your own journey in organizing. How do these kinds of events create new possibilities for organizing and building communities of care? What are some of their limitations?

2.   Mariame and Kelly write: "We believe in caring for each other as a form of cultural rebellion" (59). What do they mean? Do you agree? What connection can you make to your own orientation and practice of care?

3.   What stands out to you about Asha AE's story of offering care and aid to protesters in Chicago (62–64)?

4.   Tony Alvarado-Rivera of Chicago Freedom School says, "In organizing, especially with young people of color, it's about making sure that they have a space where they know that they are protected, where they are cared for and loved, no matter what" (65). Are there spaces like CFS in your community? In your organizing work? What would it take to build these spaces—or more of them?

5.   Pay close attention to how Alvarado-Rivera and his comrades responded when the police arrived at the Chicago Freedom School (67–70). What norms were in place that enabled them to care for the young people at the school and limit the damage the police could inflict? To what extent have you and your co-organizers made plans for how you will engage with the police? [See Appendix B, 243–244]

6.   Consider the example of Edgewater Mutual Aid. How does it illustrate how mutual aid can "create political possibilities beyond the bounds of what people generally associate with community care" (71)?

7. Of the onset of the COVID-19 pandemic preceding the George Floyd uprising, Shane Burley says, "There was a mass orientation of mutual aid to one crisis...which then made the structures logical and accessible for the next crisis" (74). Think about the work you're currently involved in. What structures are you building (or do you want to build) now to have available during the next crisis?

8. Kelly and Mariame write: "Care-driven organizing confounds the logics that are deployed to perpetuate wars, whether against a nation-state, against terrorism, or against 'crime'" (76). How does the work you are doing (or imagining doing) fit this description? Is it antiwar work? Why or why not?

9.　What additional questions came up for you as you read?

Take-it-with-you line:

What is a line from this chapter that you want to share with others? Why?

CHAPTER FOUR
THINK LIKE A GEOGRAPHER

PREREADING JOURNAL PROMPT

Before reading the chapter spend some time with its title. A couple of definitions of geography:

1. "a science that deals with the description, distribution, and interaction of the diverse physical, biological, and cultural features of the earth's surface" (Merriam-Webster)

2. "the study of the physical features of the earth and its atmosphere, and of human activity as it affects and is affected by these, including the distribution of populations and resources, land use, and industries" (Google)

Write, draw, paint, write a song or poem: *What might it mean to "think like a geographer" about the place(s) you live, work, organize, struggle, play, learn, etc.?*

REFLECTION QUESTIONS

1.   Ruth Wilson Gilmore says thinking like a geographer can "help people see, pull back the veil that makes something that's social seem natural, and something that is sometimes natural seem social" (80). What does this mean to you? What are some examples of things that seem natural, but are actually social?

2.   Stevie Wilson explores the value of zines in enabling the "subversive act" of reading in prison (83). What is your experience with reading, political activation, and education? How do you share insights, information, history, and analysis with others? What reading practices and habits do you find most generative? What do you struggle with around reading?

3.   Complete the quotation exercise outlined on page 85 and share your discoveries with your co-strugglers and comrades:

Pick out a quotation that has had a deep impact on your politics. Write it down. Now let's elaborate on its context. What injustice was being challenged? What did the speaker want most immediately? Was the quote part of a statement to the press, a line from a speech or a book, or a comment to a friend? Was it in a letter from a jailhouse? Who was the president of the United States when these words were spoken? What was the economy like? Who might have disagreed with this quote at the time it was spoken, both within and outside of social movements? If the quote is from a book, have you read it? If not, is it possible these words are calling you on a journey?

4.   Does Wilson Gilmore's description of an "extractive" (86) approach to reading resonate with you? What about her possible alternative approach—reading as if we are actors?

5.   What lessons about organizing, information, and political education most stand out to you in the example of Lucy Parsons Labs (87–90) and the police murder of Adam Toledo?

lucyparsonslabs.com

6.   Mariame and Kelly describe both the limits and possibilities of "digital methods of mobilization." What has been your experience with online political education and mobilization? What kinds of communication and social media do you and your comrades already use? What are some alternative forms of communication and information sharing you might experiment with in the future?

7.   Analyze the organizing and activism of the Chicago Alliance for Waterfront Safety (CAWS) in the context of this chapter's title: "Think Like a Geographer." In what ways did the CAWS organizers think like geographers? How did that kind of thinking inform their organizing and activism?

8.   What additional questions came up for you as you read?

Take-it-with-you line:

What is a line from this chapter that you want to share with others? Why?

CHAPTER FIVE
REJECTING CYNICISM AND BUILDING BROADER MOVEMENTS

PREREADING JOURNAL PROMPT

What is something ignorant or offensive that is said by others about the issue(s) you're organizing around? Get off your chest what you want to say in response. *Make a list. Write a tirade. Talk back. Skewer their ignorance in a political cartoon or song.*

REFLECTION QUESTIONS

1.   Why, according to the authors, is it "important to understand the distinction between activists, organizers, and political hobbyists" (98)? What are those distinctions and how do they apply to your context?

2.   Mariame and Kelly write: "As organizers, when we find ourselves correcting people's ignorance we should ask ourselves what we are inviting those people to do. What are we directing them toward?" (100). In other words, organizing requires that we shift into a different gear from the one we were in when we responded to the prereading journal prompt for this chapter. How have you and your co-strugglers responded to misunderstandings or misrepresentations with an invitation toward deeper understanding? How might you in the future?

3.   Spend a few minutes responding to the questions on pages 101 and 102. Pay attention to which of these questions is the easiest for you to answer, and which is the most difficult. If you are reading with your comrades and co-strugglers, share your answers, and note where there is disagreement and/or uncertainty that you'll need to return to as you develop your approach.

4.   Kelly and Mariame write: "Effective organizers emphasize the connections between struggles, instead of making totalizing comparisons" (104). How is the issue you are organizing around connected to other struggles? Is the work you are doing drawing connections between those struggles? If so, how? If not, what makes it hard to draw those connections?

5.   "Movement education is, in part, a deprogramming process" (105). What is your response to this sentence? To what degree does it match your experience of learning about the issues you're currently organizing around?

6. What additional questions came up for you as you read?

Take-it-with-you line:

What is a line from this chapter that you want to share with others? Why?

CHAPTER SIX
'VIOLENCE' IN SOCIAL MOVEMENTS

PREREADING JOURNAL PROMPT

Recall some acts of protest from the last several years—they do not not need to be actions you participated in or even from your community. Choose one you admire. *Imagine you are writing a letter of solidarity and appreciation to the organizers: what do you want to uplift and celebrate? What questions do you have? What will you borrow from this example?*

REFLECTION QUESTIONS

1.   What examples come to mind when the authors write, "We are surrounded by violence in this society, even under conditions that government authorities would characterize as 'peaceful,' because violence has always been embedded in the norms and functions of this system" (109)? Where do you see instances of this type of violence in your own community?

2. If, as Mariame and Kelly state, it is "imperative that the state not be the arbiter of what violence means among people seeking justice" (111), then organizers must have their own political and ethical convictions about what is and is not permissible. What convictions inform the way you think about violence?

3. Had you heard of Deona Knajdek (112) before reading this chapter? What stands out to you about her story?

4. Kelly and Mariame write, "Laws that supposedly target 'terrorists' will always be used to target activists" (116). What do you understand to be the authors' reasoning for this claim? How have you observed the concept of "terrorism" being used in your lifetime?

5. This chapter is full of actions by activists—land and water defenders, rescuers, poets —deemed "violent" by the state. Make a list of them. What do you notice? What can you learn about how the label "violent" is used? How might those lessons apply to your work and organizing?

6. What additional questions came up for you as you read?

Take-it-with-you line:

What is a line from this chapter that you want to share with others? Why?

CHAPTER SEVEN
DON'T PEDESTAL ORGANIZERS

PREREADING JOURNAL PROMPT

Reflect on your political stances over the past 5-10 years. What are some ideas, assumptions, beliefs, or predictions that you once had but now realize were wrong or misguided? *How do you view the ongoing process of learning and transformation, of refining and expanding your political convictions and practices?*

REFLECTION QUESTIONS

1. What are the dangers and traps of putting organizers on pedestals?

2. Consider your own context or organizing spaces you have observed. Have you witnessed the sudden rise in visibility of a particular organizer or activist? Reflect on the perils and possibilities of the increased visibility that can come with public speaking and social media. If you have not already, might you and your co-strugglers have a conversation to prepare for those perils and possibilities?

3. Barbara Ransby says praise of individual organizers can become "corrosive" (133). What does she mean? What is your experience with praise—both as a giver and receiver?

4.   What are the attributes of principled, "good-faith" critique (134–135)? How do you and your co-strugglers practice self-reflection and organizational reflection—or do you? What have been the outcomes, benefits, and challenges of these attempts?

5.   What is the difference between praise and appreciation? What are some concrete ways you and your comrades build a healthy culture of recognition and affirmation into your organizing work? If none currently exist, how might you develop these practices, while avoiding pedestalling?

6.   Carefully read Page May's discussion of the necessity of community in organizing (135–138). What are the key elements of the blueprint for organizing she offers and how do these apply to your work and community?

7.   What does it mean to you to be "grounded"? What kinds of organizational norms might make it more likely for you and your co-strugglers to stay grounded, in your shared work, in the community, and in each other?

8.   What additional questions came up for you as you read?

Take-it-with-you line:

What is a line from this chapter that you want to share with others? Why?

CHAPTER EIGHT
HOPE AND GRIEF
CAN CO-EXIST

PREREADING JOURNAL PROMPT

Think about some of the losses that have shaped your life. *What opportunities did you have to grieve? What demands did grief make of you? What did you learn about yourself or others through the process of grieving? How, if at all, does that grief show up in your everyday life? In your relationship-building? In your organizing?*

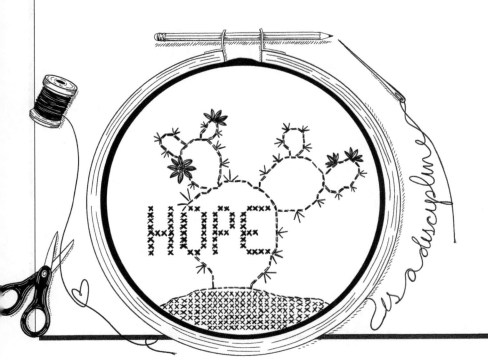

REFLECTION QUESTIONS

1. The authors write, "Our oppressors...are hoping that the battery of catastrophes we witness in real-time will shorten our attention spans until the fallen are forgotten in the blink of an eye" (152). How might you and your co-strugglers create rituals of pausing, feeling, and remembering to honor those who have been lost or taken?

2. Morning Star Gali invokes the principle of acting in the present with concern for the next seven generations (156).

3. Spend five quiet minutes sketching or writing about the world you are working toward for the children seven generations after you.

4.   After five minutes, reflect and share: What was that like? Hard? Surprising? Enlightening?

5.   Anoa J. Changa says, "In organizing, the odds are always stacked against you. That's always been the way. So you find a window. And if the window is small, you still aim for it. And you go" (163). What windows have existed for you in the past? What is your current window? How are they similar or different?

6.   Organizer Juliana Pino focuses on issues of environmental justice and insists that all forms of structural violence are connected. How does her work in Little Village (163–172) reflect that understanding? What can you learn from these organizing examples?

7.   Pino asks, "How are we waging acts of care? What is our own practice of care? How are we making sure that the community is cared for?" (171). Do you consider the work you are doing care work? Why or why not?

8.   Read Lea Kayali's description of joining a Palestinian folk dance troupe (174). Her participation in a community-based dance practice operates as both a political commitment and self-care. Reflect on your own life. Do you have practices and pastimes that represent both your political commitment and self-care? Might you reach for some opportunities like this in the future?

9.   The authors implore us to "cherish poetry, which has always played an important role in fueling hope and making space for grief in movements" (180). What is your relationship to poetry? Is it already a source of inspiration and insight for you? Or are you new to poetry? Is there a poem about grief or hope that you would like to share with others? If not, consider asking a comrade or friend for a poetry recommendation and see where it leads you.

10. What additional questions came up for you as you read?

Take-it-with-you line:

What is a line from this chapter that you want to share with others? Why?

CHAPTER NINE
ORGANIZING ISN'T MATCHMAKING

PREREADING JOURNAL PROMPT

Think about your own experiences navigating disagreements with friends, comrades, group members. Choose one example to think deeply about. *What did you learn about yourself and others through this moment of conflict and disagreement?*

REFLECTION QUESTIONS

1.   What does it mean to strive to create "movements rather than clubhouses" (182)? How might this idea apply, specifically and practically, in your own organizing?

2.   What do you recognize in Aly Wane's story (183–187), either in yourself or in organizing spaces you have been or are currently a part of?

3.   Wane says that making distinctions between what to bring to and express in which spaces helped him build his capacity as an organizer. What processing spaces (organizing, journaling, therapy, social media, etc.) are available to you and how do you use them differently?

4.   Kelly and Mariame write, "Many people describe themselves as good listeners. In reality, most people are not" (189). What struggles do you have with listening? What does the skill of authentic listening involve? What listening intentions might you set for yourself to work on?

5.   Mariame and Kelly explain, "As part of the Rogers Park Young Women's Action Team's circles, everyone had their turn to read, to speak, and to listen" (191). How might you build a practice of deliberative role shifting (reader, speaker, listener, etc.) into your meeting norms? If you already have a similar practice, what can be refined? If you are reading on your own, explore your past experience with group norms—what has worked and not worked?

6.   The authors write, "The terms and jargon we use today do not represent an 'arrival' at the 'correct' words that were always out there, waiting to be found..." (192). What's your reaction to this statement? What's been your experience learning and adapting to new language and terminology? [See Glossary, 247–250]

7.   Ejeris Dixon explores the need to make organizing spaces that include room for imperfection and questioning (193–195). Think about a time you made—or witnessed someone make—a mistake. How was it handled by you or others? What would you want to replicate or do differently in the future? Analyze your own organizing space—is there sufficient room for mistake-making? If not, how might that space be encouraged and built?

8.   What additional questions came up for you as you read?

Take-it-with-you line:

What is a line from this chapter that you want to share with others? Why?

CHAPTER TEN
AVOIDING BURNOUT AND GOING THE DISTANCE

Write or sketch: *What does burnout feel like? Sound like? Taste like? Smell like? Act like? How does it manifest in your thoughts and actions?* You can draw from your own individual experience or elaborate on what you have witnessed in others.

REFLECTION QUESTIONS

1.   Do an inventory of yourself and your organizing spaces for a "culture of martyrdom" (200). Where do you see examples of such a culture manifesting? What might you do with this inventory? How might you use it as a springboard to adaptation?

2.   Sharon Lungo of Indigenous People's Power Project says she wishes "that more people had reminded me that it was OK to gift myself things, and take pleasure in things…" (201). How are you building in reminders to yourself and each other that you deserve—as all people do—time for "care, healing, and recovery" (203)? What are some of the ways you have made that time in the past and/or may do so in the future?

ip3action.org

3.   Lungo warns that focusing on "something big or monumental" can dangerously eclipse the "everyday work that you do with each other and other humans" (204). How does her idea of an "off-season" (205) and Carlos Saavedra's metaphor of "seasonality" (211) land with you? How does it apply to your past experiences?

4.   Kelly and Mariame write, "Relief teams and mechanisms can be created at the group or organizational level, around particular organizing tasks or roles, or at the personal level, when an organizer stretched thin needs help with basic life tasks, like cooking, childcare, or picking up groceries" (207). In your setting, are there roles that are currently filled by one person that could be shared by a team? If so, how might you create structures of support and relief to care for them and avoid burnout?

CARLOS SAAVEDRA'S: Seasons c

WINTER: rejuvenate / hybernate

SUMMER: go, go, go / constant action

Response Periods

SPRING: open up / do more things / build capacity

FALL: celebrate /breakdown/reset/prep for winter

5. Sit with and respond to the questions on page 209.

- Is there a place that makes you feel whole or revived in some way?
- How often are you able to inhabit that space?
- If that space is inaccessible, what ritual or experience brings you closest to it?
- What practices or experiences help you experience a sense of renewal?
- Are these practices an ongoing part of your life?

6. Spend some time considering Carlos Saavedra's metaphor of "seasonality" (210–212). What season—Spring, Summer, Winter, or Fall—are you and your co-strugglers in right now? Or are you in a period of transition? How do you know?

7. What additional questions came up for you as you read?

Take-it-with-you line:

What is a line from this chapter that you want to share with others? Why?

CONCLUSION:
"RELATIONSHIPS, RECIPROCITY, AND STRUGGLE"
KELLY HAYES

REFLECTION QUESTION

Kelly writes, "In a world that is breaking down our connections, isolating us, and sub-siloing us to death, life-giving relationships are our best hope" (222). How does the story of how Kelly came to know (and build a friendship with) Bresha Meadows illustrate the "life-giving" properties of relationships? What do you want to hold on to from this story?

Take-it-with-you line:

What is a line from this chapter that you want to share with others? Why?

CONCLUSION: "BEYOND DOOM, TOWARD COLLECTIVE ACTION"
MARIAME KABA

REFLECTION QUESTION

Mariame builds this conclusion around a rich collection of quotations from Elizabeth Alexander, Dennis Brutus, Archbishop Desmond Tutu, Victoria Safford, Dionne Brand, Octavia Butler, and more. What can we learn from Mariame's quilting together of other people's words of wisdom—both from the words themselves and from the process of gathering them together? What voices, stories, and words are present in your own "quilting?"

Take-it-with-you line:

What is a line from this chapter that you want to share with others? Why?

AFTERWORD:
"MOVEMENTS MAKE LIFE"
HARSHA WALIA

REFLECTION QUESTION

1. Walia says that for her, *Let This Radicalize You* distills three key points:

    - Organizing is the antidote to despair.
    - Collective liberation necessitates collective care.
    - We need each other.

    Reflect on each of these points. What do they mean to you? How did your ideas about them expand or transform through engaging with this book?

2.   Add a fourth "key point" to Walia's list: what is another critical takeaway you want to hold on to from the stories and wisdom shared in this book?

Take-it-with-you line:

What is a line from this chapter that you want to share with others? Why?

A CLOSING INVITATION

As noted at the opening of this guide, reading a book can be a transformative process. If reading *Let This Radicalize You* has transformed or clarified your understanding of organizing—your efforts in the past, your practices in the present, or how you will approach future endeavors—it might be worth taking some time to crystalize what you want to carry forward from this book. Some possibilities:

1.   Create a one-pager (graphic notes) for the book. (Some beautiful examples from Project NIA and Interrupting Criminalization might inspire you.)

www.abolitionist.tools	project-nia.org	interruptingcriminalization.com

2.   Start a document called, "Ten (or So) Things I Do Not Want to Forget from *Let This Radicalize You.*" Flip (or scroll) back through the book and pull out the big "ahas" for you.

3.   Write a letter to a friend or comrade who has not read the book and share with them what you loved, what moved you, and what questions you continue to chew on. (Make sure to make a copy of the letter for yourself.)

Reading a book is a life event—it takes time, focus, energy. What gift might you offer to your future self and others related to reading *Let This Radicalize You*?

REFLECTING ON IDEAS

Reflect on the ideas articulated below: What do they spark for you? Think about what you would add, what you disagree with, what resonates for you. Jot down your thoughts in the space provided.

Organizing is the process of building power as a group and using this power to create positive change in people's lives (including our own).

ORGANIZING RESOURCE LIBRARY: https://bit.ly/OrganizingLibrary

Any politics has to be an engaged politics, not a formula.

We have to rely on the relationships that we have and build to pursue the politics that we want.

To organize effectively, you must develop your skills and increase your endurance.

There is a new set of contradictions produced by winning.

Struggle produces politics. Politics don't "just happen."

People do not experience systems.

"First, 'the system' -or those aspects of the system that people experience and perceive- loses legitimacy....Second, people who are ordinarily fatalistic, who believe that existing arrangements are inevitable, begin to assert their 'rights' that imply demands for change. Third, there is a new sense of efficacy; people who ordinarily consider themselves helpless come to believe that they have some capacity to alter their lot."

— Source: https://notesonatheory.wordpress.com/2021/03/26/telling-people-things-are-bad-is-not-enough/

"To fulfill her task of building organizations and a broader movement, the conscious organizer must be guided in her work by her answers to basic questions: What's the nature of the system? What are the current conditions within this system? And what are the forces that have the interest and the capability to make change?"

—Towards Land, Work, & Power.

"There is one thing you have got to learn about our movement. Three people are better than no people." —Fanny Lou Hamer

"You can't start a movement, but you can prepare for one." —Vincent Harding

SELF-REFLECTIONS FOR ORGANIZERS

Good leaders are accountable to a community. This list of questions Kelly created can serve as a tool for organizers to check in with themselves about whether they are practicing accountable leadership.

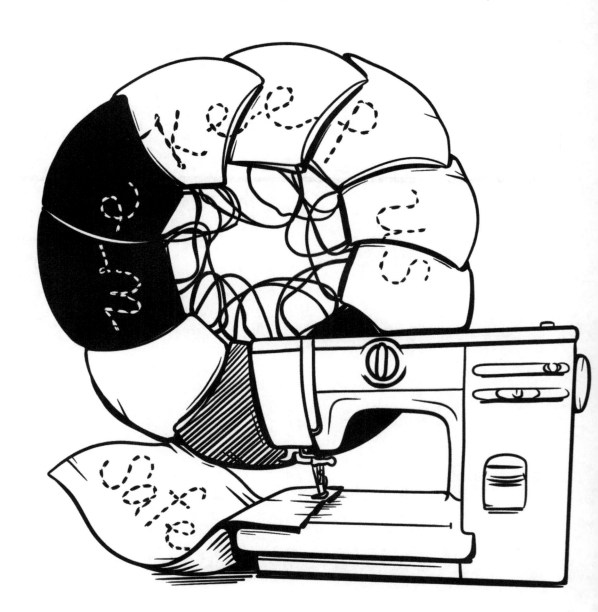

1. Who am I accountable to?

2. What community consents to my leadership when I assume it?

3. How do those interactions function?

4. Am I sure the people I'm accountable to have a traversable path to intervention/interruption/dialogue, when they feel differently than I do?

5. Who helps me reel myself in when I assume harmful attitudes, or replicate structural oppressions, internally or externally?

6. Who do I turn to for counsel/support in holding myself accountable when I have caused harm?

7. Do I acknowledge that we all both experience and cause harm?

8. Do I believe that mass movements are grounded in relationships, and if so, am I working to build those relationships, or simply attempting to enforce ideas?

MOVEMENT ASSESSMENT RESOURCES

It's always helpful to think about our work in a broader context. Mariame participated in a mutual aid workshop that was organized by the Highlander Center on May 14, 2020. This was a couple of weeks before George Floyd was killed by a cop. It was interesting to have reflected together on the questions below just a few short weeks before our social context drastically shifted. The experience underscored the importance of consistently assessing how our movements are doing.

Think about our current movement context. How would you respond to the questions below today?:

How do you describe the "new normal?"

What have we [activists/organizers] built in this moment?

- Infrastructure
- Nonmaterial infrastructure
- Relationships
- New ways of meeting people

What are the threats/crises?

- New
- Existing
- Foreseeable

Where should we maintain our work? What should we move forward with?

Where should we build/invest/create for the next crisis?

What is our story? Individually/communally/regionally/metro/rural/nationally/internationally

It's important to plan for conflict because it is common in movement work and in organizing. It's to be expected and it is not a sign of failure. Below are some helpful resources for addressing movement conflict(s). Read through these so you're not surprised by it and so you can embrace conflict as a generative aspect of activism and organizing.

"When We Fall Apart"   interruptingcriminalization.com/when-we-fall-apart

"In It Together"   interruptingcriminalization.com/in-it-together

DIRECT ACTIONS

Kelly has spent many years engaging in direct action and also in teaching direct action tactics and strategy. Below is some wisdom gleaned from her experiences.

Why do we organize direct actions?

- **To build power within the arc of a strategic campaign**
  Campaign-based actions should escalate over time and move the campaign closer to its goal.

- **To mark a momentous occasion, such as an anniversary, an assassination, a major political convention, or a larger call to action.**

- **As acts of political communion, to reaffirm our commitment to each other and to our values.**
  Some actions are primarily about sustaining our revolutionary spirit and remembering who we are.

- **Direct actions can also address community needs in a manner that is inherently political.**
  Such acts often involve acts of mutual aid that are criminalized or otherwise discouraged by the state.

Have you participated in actions that reflect each of these motivations? Did some embody more than one of these objectives?

Direct action tells a story. So when we look at a protest, it should be clear what it's communicating to us. Can a stranger walking by tell what it's about? Kelly often tells activists to imagine the photo they want on the front page of a newspaper. Think about the last protest you attended. Was the story being told clear and visible? If not, what could participants have done differently to make their message more apparent? What imagery might you invoke at your next protest to better tell your story?

On Accountability in Direct Action

Direct actions often create disruptive, high-stress situations, and the stakes can be high, both physically and emotionally. So it is crucial to recognize in advance that participants will sometimes say or do the wrong thing. And we will sometimes disappoint each other. If a group plans to organize actions together, particularly on a continuous basis, it is essential that they acknowledge up front that harm will likely happen and that people will make mistakes.

What does accountability look like in the group you are working with?

Do we understand that direct action is imperfect and messy?

Are we willing to start with compassion when we are frustrated with each other?

Sometimes debriefs get ugly. Are we willing to take a nonpunitive approach to resolving conflict?

ACTIVIST/ORGANIZER WISDOM

Wisdom from longtime organizer Fahd Ahmed:

Of course it's a given that the rightwing narrows everything down to individual choices/bootstraps/etc. |But the left (in the US) dissonantly focuses either only on structures and systems, rendering an absolute structural determinism...or alternatively presents its own logics of individualism.

The reality:

Systems and structures dominate

But as human beings we have choices/decisions/agency

As individuals those choices are limited (yet important)

And collectively (with discipline) our choices add up to a force(s)

Clarity and precision on each of these points reflects distinctly different philosophies, with significant implications...

[Source: Facebook post, May 26, 2020]

Right: Image by Kah Yangni

"SYSTEMS and STRUCTURES DOMINATE But as HUMAN BEINGS. WE HAVE CHOICES as INDIVIDUALS THOSE CHOICES are LIMITED. BUT COLLECTIVELY our CHOICES ADD UP to A FORCE".

~FAHD AHMED

KAHYANGNI 2020

More Organizer Wisdom

We asked what veteran activists and organizers would have appreciated in a workbook when they were starting out. We also invited those newer to activism and organizing about what they wish they had in a workbook to support them in their work. We're sharing some of their responses here.

Cofounder of Survived & Punished, organizer Stacy Suh:

1. Being able to discern what is your responsibility as an organizer to own and hold for others; what are expectations that are being implicitly put on you that aren't actually your responsibilities?

2. Not falling into the trap of false urgency. How do you move at your own speed and practice your values in the organizing work, rather than meeting obligations/demands that others put on you? (Alternatively, how do we leverage rapid response moments/galvanizing moments to get more people involved in our work in the long run?)

3. Understanding your own style/strengths as an organizer and there's no one way to be an effective organizer. I feel that the role of the 'organizer' has been glorified over the years, and feel like that's not necessary... And also recognizing that it is okay not to be an organizer and that we can play other roles in the movement too.

4. Defining what 'building power' means to you and what that looks like—what kind of power? (Is it economic power? Political power? People power? Something else?) How do you measure it?

5. 'We can do anything but not everything'—being disciplined about what we prioritize, be able to clearly articulate why we prioritize certain projects/goals over others. Also thinking more carefully about sequencing different projects and goals so that they can be more effective.

Organizer Rachael Zafer:

If I had used a workbook way back when, I would have benefited from some questions that encouraged me to think about how and where I was feeling the work (the connection, the learning, the struggle) in my body and in my heart. Understanding organizing as interconnected with how we feel inside ourselves was a pivotal point of transformation for me. I also would have benefited from probing into how, as an introvert, I could offer just as much as the person holding the mic.

Organizer Meg Groves:

I wish I had known: Don't allow yourself to be pushed around by people who are equally as in/experienced as you but just louder/more confident; and don't conflate tactics with strategy.

Organizer Debbie Southorn:

I think something about how it's okay to start small. I think new folks sometimes have so much internalized pressure to be big immediately and are upset if 30 people don't come to their first meeting. And remembering that starting with a crew that's small but aligned is how we can grow our impact, instead of starting big and being a giant mess lol.

Zine by Ricardo Levins Morales:

Lessons for Organizing by Ricardo Levins Morales

bit.ly/OrganizingLessons

BIBLIOGRAPHY

The following are books and texts that we think are useful for new organizers and activists. They offer valuable insights, information, and inspiration. We've selected texts that can be read on your own but that are also good to read and discuss with other people. Importantly, this is not a definitive list but rather a starting point as you begin to deepen your knowledge and skills as an organizer and activist. There are so many more excellent books to read that we didn't include.

Essays/Memoir/Speeches

Andaiye. *The Point Is to Change the World: Selected Writings of Andaiye.* Edited by D. Alissa Trotz. London: Pluto Press, 2020.

brown, adrienne maree. *Emergent Strategy: Shaping Change, Changing Worlds.* Chico, CA: AK Press, 2017.

Cabral, Amílcar. *Unity and Struggle: Speeches and Writings.* New York: Monthly Review Press, 1979.

Horton, Myles, Judith Kohl, and Herbert Kohl. *The Long Haul: An Autobiography.* New York: Teachers College Press, 1997.

Horton, Myles and Paulo Freire. *We Make the Road by Walking: Conversations on Education and Social Change.* Edited by Brenda Bell, John Gaventa, and John Peters. Philadelphia: Temple University Press, 1990.

Johnson, Ayana Elizabeth, and Katharine K. Wilkinson, eds. *All We Can Save: Truth, Courage, and Solutions for the Climate Crisis.* New York: One World, 2020.

Kelley, Robin D. G.. *Freedom Dreams: The Black Radical Imagination.* Twentieth anniversary ed. Boston: Beacon Press, 2022.

Maynard, Robyn, and Leanne Betasamosake Simpson. *Rehearsals for Living*. Chicago: Haymarket Books, 2022.

Melrod, Jon. *Fighting Times: Organizing on the Front Lines of the Class War*. Oakland: PM Press, 2022.

Milstein, Cindy, ed. *Rebellious Mourning: The Collective Work of Grief*. Chico, CA: AK Press, 2017.

Palumbo-Liu, David. *Speaking out of Place: Getting Our Political Voices Back*. Chicago: Haymarket Books, 2021.

Rodney, Walter. *The Groundings with My Brothers*. Chicago: Research Associates School Times Publications, 1990.

Taylor, Astra. *Remake the World: Essays, Reflections, Rebellions*. Chicago: Haymarket Books, 2021.

Turshen, Julia. *Feed the Resistance: Recipes + Ideas for Getting Involved*. San Francisco: Chronicle Books, 2017.

Zinn, Howard. *You Can't Be Neutral on a Moving Train: A Personal History*. 2002. Updated edition with foreword by Keeanga-Yamhatta Taylor, Boston: Beacon Press, 2018.

Organizing Stories

Engler, Mark, and Paul Engler. *This Is an Uprising: How Nonviolent Revolt Is Shaping the Twenty-First Century*. New York: Nation Books, 2017.

Fithian, Lisa. *Shut It down: Stories from a Fierce, Loving Resistance*. White River Junction, VT: Chelsea Green Publishing, 2019.

Jaffe, Sarah. *Necessary Trouble: Americans in Revolt*. New York: Nation Books, 2016.

Jha, Sandhya Rani. *Transforming Communities: How People Like You Are Healing Their Neighborhoods*. St. Louis: Chalice Press, 2017.

Kauffman, L. A. *Direct Action: Protest and the Reinvention of American Radicalism*. London: Verso, 2017.

McAlevey, Jane. *No Shortcuts: Organizing for Power in the New Gilded Age*. New York: Oxford University Press, 2016.

Pitkin, Daisy. *On the Line: A Story of Class, Solidarity, and Two Women's Epic Fight to Build a Union*. Chapel Hill, NC: Algonquin Books of Chapel Hill, 2022.

Sen, Rinku. *Stir It up: Lessons in Community Organizing and Advocacy*. San Francisco: Jossey-Bass, 2003.

Solnit, Rebecca. *A Paradise Built in Hell: The Extraordinary Communities That Arise in Disasters*. New York: Viking Penguin, 2009.

Midcentury Black Freedom Movement Histories

Dittmer, John. *Local People: The Struggle for Civil Rights in Mississippi*. Urbana: University of Illinois Press, 1995.

Kelley, Robin D. G. *Hammer and Hoe: Alabama Communists during the Great Depression*. Chapel Hill: University of North Carolina Press, 1990.

Payne, Charles M. *I've Got the Light of Freedom: The Organizing Tradition and the Mississippi Freedom Struggle*. 1995. Revised edition with new preface, Berkeley: University of California Press, 2007.

Ransby, Barbara. *Ella Baker and the Black Freedom Movement: A Radical Democratic Vision*. Chapel Hill: University of North Carolina Press, 2003.

Siracusa, Anthony C. *Nonviolence Before King: The Politics of Being and the Black Freedom Struggle*. Chapel Hill: The University of North Carolina Press, 2021.

Theoharis, Jeanne. *The Rebellious Life of Mrs. Rosa Parks: Young Readers' Edition*. Adapted by Brandy Colbert and Jeanne Theoharis. Boston: Beacon Press, 2021.

Zinn, Howard. SNCC, *The New Abolitionists*. 1964. Reprint, Boston: South End Press, 2002.

Research/Theory/History

Arruzza, Cinzia, Tithi Bhattacharya, and Nancy Fraser. *Feminism for the 99 Percent: A Manifesto*. London: Verso, 2019.

Berger, Dan, and Emily K. Hobson, eds. *Remaking Radicalism: A Grassroots Documentary Reader of the United States, 1973-2001*. Athens, GA: University of Georgia Press, 2020.

Browne, Jaron, Marisa Franco, Jason Negrón-Gonzales, and Steve Williams. *Towards Land, Work & Power*. Tenth anniversary ed. Oakland: Unite to Fight Press, 2016.

Cantarow, Ellen, Susan Gushee O'Mally, and Sharon Hartman Strom. *Moving the Mountain: Women Working for Social Change*. New York: Feminist Press, 1980.

Chomsky, Aviva, and Steve Striffler, eds. *Organizing for Power: Building a Twenty-First Century Labor Movement in Boston*. Chicago: Haymarket Books, 2021.

Clover, Joshua. *Riot. Strike. Riot.: The New Era of Uprisings*. London: Verso, 2016.

Davis, Angela Y., Gina Dent, Erica R. Meiners, and Beth E. Richie. *Abolition. Feminism. Now*. Chicago: Haymarket Books, 2022.

Ganz, Marshall. *Why David Sometimes Wins: Leadership, Organization, and Strategy in the California Farm Worker Movement*. Oxford: Oxford University Press, 2010.

Haiven, Max, and Alex Khasnabish. *The Radical Imagination: Social Movement Research in the Age of Austerity*. London: Zed Books, 2014.

Han, Hahrie. *How Organizations Develop Activists: Civic Associations and Leadership in the 21st Century*. Oxford: Oxford University Press, 2014.

Hogan, Wesley C. *On the Freedom Side: How Five Decades of Youth Activists Have Remixed American History*. Chapel Hill: University of North Carolina Press, 2019.

INCITE!, ed. *The Revolution Will Not Be Funded: Beyond the Non-Profit Industrial Complex*. Duke University Press, 2007.

Orleck, Annelise. *Storming Caesars Palace: How Black Mothers Fought Their Own War on Poverty*. Boston: Beacon Press, 2005.

Pineda, Erin R. *Seeing like an Activist: Civil Disobedience and the Civil Rights Movement*. New York: Oxford University Press, 2021.

Schulman, Sarah. *Let the Record Show: A Political History of ACT UP New York, 1987-1993*. New York: Farrar, Straus and Giroux, 2021.

Walia, Harsha. *Undoing Border Imperialism*. Chico, CA: AK Press/Institute for Anarchist Studies, 2013.

Wood, Ellen M. *The Origin of Capitalism: A Longer View*. London: Verso, 2017.

Manuals/Handbooks

Alinsky, Saul David. *Rules for Radicals: A Practical Primer for Realistic Radicals*. 1971. Vintage Books ed. New York: Vintage Books, 1989.

bergman, carla, Hari Alluri, and Nick Montgomery. *Joyful Militancy: Building Thriving Resistance in Toxic Times*. Chico, CA: AK Press/Institute for Anarchist Studies, 2017. Available via theanarchistlibrary.org: https://theanarchistlibrary.org/library/joyful-militancy-bergman-montgomery.

Bishop, Anne. *Becoming an Ally: Breaking the Cycle of Oppression in People*, 3rd ed. Halifax: Fernwood Publishing, 2015.

Bobo, Kimberley A., Jackie Kendall, and Steve Max. *Organizing for Social Change: Midwest Academy Manual for Activists*. 4th ed. Santa Ana, CA: The Forum Press, 2010.

Boyd, Andrew, and Dave Oswald Mitchell, eds. *Beautiful Trouble: A Toolbox for Revolution*. New York: OR Books, 2016.

brown, adrienne maree. *Holding Change: The Way of Emergent Strategy Facilitation and Mediation*. Chico, CA: AK Press, 2021.

Brown, Michael Jacoby. *Building Powerful Community Organizations: A Personal Guide to Creating Groups That Can Solve Problems and Change the World*. Arlington, MA: Long Haul Press, 2006.

105

Foster, William Z. *Organizing Methods in the Steel Industry*. New York: Workers Library Publishers, Inc., 1936. Available via marxistslibrary. org:https://www.marxists.org/archive/foster/1936/10/organizing-methods-steel-industry/index.htm.

Iyer, Deepa. *Social Change Now: A Guide for Reflection and Connection*. Washington, DC: Thick Press, 2022.

Kaufman, Cynthia. *The Sea Is Rising and so Are We: A Climate Justice Handbook*. Oakland, CA: PM Press, 2021.

La Botz, Dan. *A Troublemaker's Handbook: How to Fight Back Where You Work—and Win!* Detroit, MI: Labor Notes, 1991.

Mann, Eric. *Playbook for Progressives: 16 Qualities of the Successful Organizer*. Boston: Beacon Press, 2011.

Mayotte, Cliff, and Claire Kiefer, eds. *Say It Forward: A Guide to Social Justice Storytelling*. Chicago: Haymarket Books, 2018.

Reinsborough, Patrick, and Doyle Canning. *RE:Imagining Change: How to Use Story-Based Strategy to Win Campaigns, Build Movements, and Change the World*. 2nd ed. Oakland, CA: PM Press, 2017.

Ricketts, Aidan. *The Activists' Handbook: A Step-by-Step Guide to Participatory Democracy*. London: Zed Books, 2012.

Shields, Katrina, and Phil Somerville. *In the Tiger's Mouth: An Empowerment Guide for Social Action*. Philadelphia: New Society, 1994.

Smucker, Jonathan Matthew. *Hegemony How-to: A Roadmap for Radicals*. Chico, CA: AK Press, 2017.

Spade, Dean. *Mutual Aid: Building Solidarity during This Crisis (and the Next)*. London: Verso, 2020.

Thompson, Gabriel. *Calling All Radicals: How Grassroots Organizers Can Save Our Democracy*. New York: Nation Books, 2007.

Visual

Kauffman, L. A. *How to Read a Protest: The Art of Organizing and Resistance*. Oakland: University of California Press, 2018.

Light, Melanie, and Ken Light. *Picturing Resistance: Moments and Movements of Social Change from the 1950s to Today*. California: Ten Speed Press, 2020.

Siegler, Bonnie. *Signs of Resistance: A Visual History of Protest in America*. New York: Artisan, 2018.

For Youth

Chambers, Veronica. *Resist: 35 Profiles of Ordinary People Who Rose up against Tyranny and Injustice*. New York: Harper, 2018.

Gerin, Carolyn, Elisa Camahort Page, and Jamia Wilson. *Road Map for Revolutionaries: Resistance, Activism, and Advocacy for All*. California: Ten Speed Press, 2018.

Haworth-Booth, Alice, and Emily Haworth-Booth. *Protest!: How People Have Come Together to Change the World*. London: Pavilion Books, 2021.

Johnson, Maureen, ed. *How I Resist: Activism and Hope for a New Generation*. New York: Wednesday Books, 2018.

Noxon, Christopher. *Good Trouble: Lessons from the Civil Rights Playbook*. New York: Abrams, 2018.

OTHER USEFUL RESOURCES

Articles

"#2: The 500-Year Clock + Free Postcards." *One Million Experiments Newsletter*. March 2, 2023. https://millionexperiments.substack.com/p/2-the-500-year-clock-free-postcards.

"Access Suggestions for Mobilizations." *Sins Invalid* (blog). June 8, 2020. https://www.sinsinvalid.org/news-1/2020/6/8/access-suggestions-for-mobilizations.

Battistoni, Alyssa. "Spadework: On Political Organizing." *N+1*. Spring 2019. https://www.nplusonemag.com/issue-34/politics/spadework/.

Berlin, Isaiah. "A Message to the 21st Century." *NY Book Review*. October 23, 2014 https://www.nybooks.com/articles/2014/10/23/message-21st-century/.

Crass, Chris. "Organizing Lessons from Civil Rights Leader Ella Baker." *Anarkismo.net*. March 3, 2008. https://www.anarkismo.net/article/7645.

Dixon, Chris. "Organizing to Win the World: Addressing the Left's Deficit of Strategic Thinking." *Briar Patch*. March 18, 2015. https://briarpatchmagazine.com/articles/view/organizing-to-win-the-world.

Grace, Sharlyn. "Organizers Change What's Possible." *Inquest: A Decarceral Brainstorm*. September 23, 2021. https://inquest.org/organizers-change-whats-possible/.

Jaffe, Sarah. "Comment: The Power and Promise of Organizing." *The Progressive Magazine*. October 4, 2021. https://progressive.org/magazine/power-and-promise-organizing-jaffe/.

Lorde, Audre. "Commencement Address [at Oberlin College]." May 29, 1989. Published on *QueerHistory.Com*. https://queerhistory.com/radical-graduation.

Patel, Amisha. "Lessons from Chicago Coalition Building." *The Forge*. October 27, 2022. https://forgeorganizing.org/article/lessons-chicago-coalition-building.

Pitkin, Daisy. "The Gospel of Organizing." *The Baffler*. April 21, 2022. https://thebaffler.com/latest/the-gospel-of-organizing-pitkin.

Raffo, Susan. "At Least Two Layers of Support: An Anatomy of Collective Care." *SusanRaffo.com* (blog).May 13, 2021. https://www.susanraffo.com/blog/at-least-two-layers-of-support-an-anatomy-of-collective-care.

Tastrom, Katie. "10 Ways We Can Make Leadership Accessible for Sick Folks in Activism." *The Body is Not an Apology*. September 15, 2017. https://thebodyisnotanapology.com/magazine/10-ways-we-can-make-leadership-accessible-for-sick-folks/.

Toolkits

Organizing Resources Google Doc by Timmy Chau: bit.ly/41ZdEar

Get in Formation: A Community Safety Toolkit by Vision Change Win: bit.ly/VCWSafetyToolkit

Videos

A Circle By the River by Ricardo Levins Morales: youtu.be/WCJOLamgVEQ

What a Time to Be Alive by Visionary Organizing Lab: youtu.be/7An6aVfc7lc&t=1s

Building Power Sin, Contra Y Desde El Estado by Mijente: https://mijente.net/2022/04/building-power-sin-contra-y-desde-el-estado/

Podcasts

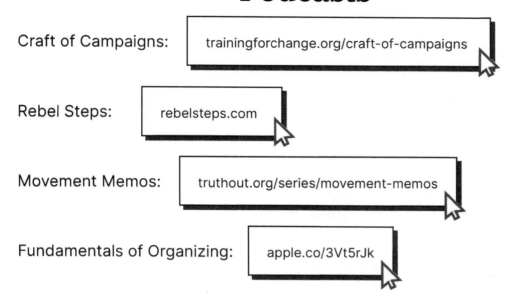

Craft of Campaigns: trainingforchange.org/craft-of-campaigns

Rebel Steps: rebelsteps.com

Movement Memos: truthout.org/series/movement-memos

Fundamentals of Organizing: apple.co/3Vt5rJk

Mutual Aid

Big Door Brigade: bigdoorbrigade.com

SOILTJP on pods: soiltjp.org/our-work/pods

Printed in the USA
CPSIA information can be obtained
at www.ICGtesting.com
JSHW051911121024
71501JS00004B/7